BABY, *BABY*

The Best Bible Names for Your Baby

A BARBOUR BOOK

© 1992 by Barbour and Company, Inc.

All Scripture quotations are from the King James Version of the Bible.

Published by **Barbour and Company, Inc.**
         P.O. Box 719
         Uhrichsville, Ohio 44683

Typeset by Typetronix, Inc., Cape Coral, Florida

ISBN 1-55748-269-1

Printed in the United States of America

1 2 3 4 5 / 97 96 95 94 93 92

A good name is rather to be chosen
than great riches.
Proverbs 22:1

Please note:
Names denoted by an asterisk (*) could be used for girls or boys.

Aaron

lofty, mountainous

Pronunciation Guide
Bible: **aharōn**
Today: **er′ən**

Is not Aaron the Levite thy brother?
Exodus 4:14

4

*A*bigail

the joy of the father

> ### Pronunciation Guide
> Bible: abīgayil
> Today: ab′ə gāl′

She was a woman of good understanding, and
of a beautiful countenance. *1 Samuel 25:3*

5

Abel

vanity, breath

> *Pronunciation Guide*
> Bible: **hebel**
> Today: $\bar{a}'$ b' l

And the Lord had respect unto Abel and to his offering.
Genesis 4:4

6

Abital/Avital

of dew

And unto David were sons born ... the fifth, ...
the son of Abital.   *2 Samuel 3:2, 4*   7

Abraham

the father of a great multitude

Pronunciation Guide	
Bible:	**'abhraham**
Today:	ā´ brə ham´

Thy name shall be Abraham; for a father of
many nations have I made thee.   *Genesis 17:5*

8

*A*dah

an ornament, beauty

> *Pronunciation Guide*
> Bible: ʻādhā
> Today: ā´də

And Adah bare Jabal: he was the father of such as dwell in tents and of such as have cattle.

Genesis 4:20 | 9

Adam

---

earthy, taken out of the red earth

> *Pronunciation Guide*
> Bible:　ādām
> Today:　ad´əm

The first man is of the earth, earthy: the second man is the Lord from heaven.
1 Corinthians 15:47

10

Adina

slender, adorned

Pronunciation Guide
Today: **ad ē′nah, ad ī′nah**

Also the valiant men of the armies were . . . Adina
. . . a captain of the Reubenites . . . .

1 Chronicles 11:26, 42 | 11 |

Adriel*

the flock of God

> *Pronunciation Guide*
>
> Today: ā′drē el

But it came to pass at the time when Merab
Saul's daughter should have been given to
David, that she was given unto Adriel ....

1 Samuel 18:19

12

A mi

mother, the head of a great family

Pronunciation Guide
Today: ay´my or ay´mē

The children of Solomon's servants . . . the children of Ami.   *Ezra 2:55, 57*

13

Alexander

defender of men

> *Pronunciation Guide*
> Bible: **Alexandros**
> Today: **al´ ig zan´der**

And they compel one Simon a Cyrenian, . . .
the father of Alexander, . . . to bear his
cross.   *Mark 15:21*

14

*Ariel**

---

lion of God

Pronunciation Guide
Bible: 'arī' ēl
Today: ar´ ē əl

Then sent I for . . . Ariel . . . .
Ezra 8:16

Amos

borne by God, weighty

> *Pronunciation Guide*
> Bible: **'āmōs**
> Today: **ā´məs**

Then answered Amos, . . . I was no prophet,
neither was I a prophet's son; but I was a
herdman, and a gatherer of sycomore fruit.
Amos 7:14

16

Anna

---

gracious, merciful

> **Pronunciation Guide**
> Bible: **hannāh**
> Today: **an′ə**

And there was one Anna, a prophetess, . . . and
she coming in that instant gave thanks likewise
unto the Lord, and spake of him to all . . . that
looked for redemption in Jerusalem.

Luke 2:36, 38 17

Andrew

strong, manly

> *Pronunciation Guide*
> Bible: **andreios**
> Today: **an´droo**

18

And Jesus, walking by the sea of Galilee,
saw . . . Simon called Peter, and Andrew
his brother, casting a net into the sea: for
they were fishers.   *Matthew 4:18*

Avah

(a city in 2 Kings 17:24)

> Pronunciation Guide
> Today: ā′vah

And the king of Assyria brought men from
Babylon, and from Cuthah, and from Avah
. . . .   *2 Kings 17:24* 19

Asher*

---

blessed, fortunate, happy

Pronunciation Guide
Today: **ash´ər**

And Leah said, Happy am I, for the daughters will call me blessed: and she called his name Asher. *Genesis 30:13*

20

Bethany

the house of song, the grace of God

> *Pronunciation Guide*
> Today: **beth´ə nē**

And he led them out as far as to Bethany, and he
lifted up his hands, and blessed them.

Luke 24:50 21

Barak

thunderbolt, lightning

Pronunciation Guide
Today: **ba´rack**

And what shall I more say? for the time
would fail me to tell of . . . Barak . . . who
through faith subdued kingdoms . . . .
                                    Hebrews 11:32-33

22

Bethel

house of God

> *Pronunciation Guide*
> Bible: **bēth 'ĕl**
> Today: **beth´əl**

And he called the name of that place Bethel:
. . . and this stone, which I have set for a
pillar, shall be God's house.

Genesis 28:19, 22 | 23 |

Barnabas

son of exhortation

> Pronunciation Guide
> Bible: **barnebhū' āh**
> Today: **bär′nə bəs**

. . . They sent forth Barnabas . . . who . . . exhorted them all, . . . for he was a good man, full of the Holy Ghost and of faith.
Acts 11:22-24

24

Cana/Kanah

zeal, a nest

Pronunciation Guide
Today: kā´nə

. . . There was a marriage in Cana of Galilee . . . *John 2:1*

25

Benjamin

son of the right hand, fortunate

> *Pronunciation Guide*
> Bible: **binyamin**
> Today: **ben´jə mən**

And of Benjamin he said, The beloved of the LORD shall dwell in safety by him; and the LORD shall cover him all the day long, and he shall dwell between his shoulders. *Deuteronomy 33:12*

26

Candace

who possesses contrition

. . . Behold, a man of Ethiopia . . . under
Candace queen of the Ethiopians, . . . had
come to Jerusalem for to worship.

Acts 8:27   27

Caleb

faithful

> *Pronunciation Guide*
> Bible: **kālēb**
> Today: **kā'leb**

And Caleb stilled the people before Moses, and said, Let us go up at once, and possess it; for we are well able to overcome it.

Numbers 13:30

28

Chloe

blooming, verdant

> *Pronunciation Guide*
> Today: **klō´ē**

For it hath been declared unto me of you, my brethren, by them which are of the house of Chloe, that there are contentions among you. *1 Corinthians 1:11*

29

Clement

mild, good, merciful

> *Pronunciation Guide*
> Today: **klem´ənt**

And I intreat thee . . . help . . . Clement
also, and with other my fellowlabourers,
whose names are in the book of life.
Philippians 4:3

30

Claudia

(a Roman woman)

> Pronunciation Guide
> Today: klô´dē ə

Eubulus greeteth thee, . . . and Claudia,
and all the brethren.   *2 Timothy 4:21*

31

Cyrus

the sun

> *Pronunciation Guide*
> Today: **sī′rus**

32

Thus saith the Lord to his anointed, to Cyrus,
whose right hand I have holden, to subdue
nations before him . . . .   *Isaiah 45:1*

*D*annah

(a city in Palestine, in the tribe of Judah)

Pronunciation Guide
Today: **dan′nah**

This is the inheritance of the tribe of the
children of Judah . . . and Dannah . . . .
Joshua 15:20, 49

33

Daniel

God is my judge

> *Pronunciation Guide*
> Bible: **dāni' ēl**
> Today: **dan'yəl**

. . . And the king spake and said to Daniel, O Daniel, servant of the living God, is thy God, whom thou servest continually, able to deliver thee from the lions? *Daniel 6:20*

34

*D*ara

---

companion, house of the shepherd

> *Pronunciation Guide*
> Today: **da´rah**

And the sons of Zerah; . . . and Dara . . . .
1 Chronicles 2:6

35

Darius

he that inquires

Pronunciation Guide

Today: də rē´əs   or   də´rē us

Then king Darius wrote unto all people, nations, and languages, . . . Peace be multiplied unto you.   *Daniel 6:25*

36

Deborah

a word, a bee

> **Pronunciation Guide**
> Bible: **debōrāh**
> Today: **deb′ər ə**

And she [Deborah] dwelt under the palm tree . . . and the children of Israel came up to her for judgment.

Judges 4:5

37

David

beloved

> *Pronunciation Guide*
> Bible: **dāvīd**
> Today: **dā´ vid**

Now he was ruddy, and withal of a beautiful countenance, and goodly to look to. And the LORD said, Arise, anoint him: for this is he.

1 Samuel 16:12

Delilah

delicate

Pronunciation Guide
Bible: **delīlāh**
Today: **di līʹlə**

And Delilah said to Samson, Tell me, I pray thee, wherein thy great strength lieth.... *Judges 16:6*

39

Demetrius

---

belonging to Demeter, fertile

Pronunciation Guide
Today: **de mē′ trē us**

Demetrius hath good report of all men,
and of the truth itself . . . .

3 John 12

Diana

luminous

Pronunciation Guide
Today: **dī an´ə**

... What man is there that knoweth not how that the city of the Ephesians is a worshipper of the great goddess Diana....

Acts 19:35

41

Eli

high

Pronunciation Guide
Bible: 'ēlī
Today: ē'lī

Then Eli called Samuel, and said, Samuel, my son. And he answered, Here am I.
1 Samuel 3:16

42

Dinah

vindicated

Pronunciation Guide
Bible: **dīnāh**
Today: **dī´nə**

And Dinah the daughter of Leah, which she bare unto Jacob, went out to see the daughters of the land. *Genesis 34:1*

Elijah

my God is Jehovah

> Pronunciation Guide
> Bible: 'ēlīyāhū
> Today: I lī'jə

Then said Elijah unto the people, I, even I only, remain a prophet of the Lord . . . .
1 Kings 18:22

44

Dorcas

gazelle

Pronunciation Guide
Today: **dor´kəs**

Now there was at Joppa a certain disciple . . .
called Dorcas: this woman was full of good
works and almsdeeds which she did.

Acts 9:36

45

Ethan

firmness, strength

> *Pronunciation Guide*
> Bible: ēthān
> Today: ē′ thən

And Solomon's wisdom excelled the wisdom . . . of Egypt. For he was wiser than ... Ethan the Ezrahite . . . .   *1 Kings 4:30-31*

46

Drusilla

watered by the dew

Pronunciation Guide
Today: **drew sil´lah**

And after certain days, . . . Felix came with
his wife Drusilla . . . .   *Acts 24:24*

47

Felix

happy

And as he [Paul] reasoned of righteousness, temperance, and judgment to come, Felix trembled . . . .   *Acts 24:25*

48

Elisabeth/Elizabeth

God is my oath

> *Pronunciation Guide*
> Bible: **elīsheba'**
> Today: **i liz'ə bəth**

. . . Thy prayer is heard; and thy wife
Elisabeth shall bear thee a son, and thou
shalt call his name John.   *Luke 1:13*

49

Gabriel

God is my strength

> *Pronunciation Guide*
> Bible: **gabhrī' ēl**
> Today: **gā´brē əl**

And the angel answering said unto him, I am Gabriel, that stand in the presence of God; and am sent to speak unto thee, and to shew thee glad tidings.   *Luke 1:19*

Elika

whom God purifies

> *Pronunciation Guide*
> Today: **el´í kah**

Elika the Harodite . . . .
2 Samuel 23:25

51

Gideon

---

one who cuts down

And the angel of the LORD appeared unto
him [Gideon], and said unto him, The LORD
is with thee, thou mighty man of valour.

Judges 6:12

52

Esther

---

star

> *Pronunciation Guide*
> Bible: **estēr**
> Today: **es´tər**

And Esther obtained favour in the sight
of all them that looked upon her.

Esther 2:15

53

Hillel

praising

Pronunciation Guide
Today: **hil´el**

And after him Abdon the son of Hillel, ...
judged Israel.   *Judges 12:13*

Eve

life

> *Pronunciation Guide*
> Bible: **hawwāh**
> Today: **ēv**

And Adam called his wife's name Eve; because she was the mother of all living. *Genesis 3:20*

55

Ira

---

watchful

> *Pronunciation Guide*
> Today: ī′rə

And Ira also the Jairite was a chief ruler about David.   *2 Samuel 20:26*

Hadassah

myrtle, joy

And he brought up Hadassah, that is
Esther, his uncle's daughter . . . .

Esther 2:7

57

Isaac

laughter

> *Pronunciation Guide*
> Bible: **yitshāq**
> Today: **ī´zək**

And it came to pass after the death of
Abraham, that God blessed his son Isaac;
and Isaac dwelt by the well Lahai-roi.

Genesis 25:11

Hagar

fl
flight

And Abraham rose up early in the morning, and took bread, and a bottle of water, and gave it unto Hagar, . . . and she departed, and wandered in the wilderness of Beer-sheba.   *Genesis 21:14*

59

Isaiah

salvation of Jehovah

> *Pronunciation Guide*
> Bible: **yĕsha 'yah**
> Today: **ī zā´ə**

Then said I, Woe is me! for I am undone;...
for mine eyes have seen the King, the Lord
of Hosts.   *Isaiah 6:5*

Hannah

gracious, merciful

Pronunciation Guide
Today: **han´** ə

And Hannah prayed, and said, My heart rejoiceth in the Lord, mine horn is exalted in the LORD . . . .   *1 Samuel 2:1*

61

Ishmael

whom God hears

And as for Ishmael, I have heard thee:
Behold, I have blessed him, and will make
him fruitful . . . I will make him a great
nation.   *Genesis 17:20*

62

Hosanna

---

save, we pray

> *Pronunciation Guide*
> Bible: **hōshī 'āh nnā**
> Today: **hō zan'ə**

... Hosanna to the son of David: Blessed is he that cometh in the name of the Lord; Hosanna in the highest.

Matthew 21:9

63

Israel

soldier of God

Pronunciation Guide
Bible: **yisrā' ēl**
Today: **iz´rā əl**

. . . . Thy name shall be called no more
Jacob, but Israel: for as a prince hast thou
power with God and with men. . . .

Genesis 32:28

64

*I*ndia

praise

> Pronunciation Guide
> Today: in´dē a

. . . Ahasuerus . . . reigned from India
even unto Ethiopia, over an hundred
and seven and twenty provinces.

Esther 1:1

65

Jacob

he that supplants

Pronunciation Guide
Bible: Ja 'aqob
Today: jā´kəb

And Jacob vowed a vow, saying, If God
will be with me, . . . so that I come again to
my father's house in peace; then shall the
LORD be my God.   *Genesis 28:20-21*

66

*J*ada

wise, knowing

> *Pronunciation Guide*
> Today: **jā´dah**

And the sons of Jada ... of Shammai....
1 Chronicles 2:28

67

Jahleel

---

hoping in God

Of the sons of Zebulun after their families:
. . . of Jahleel, the family of the Jahleelites.
Numbers 26:26

*J*anna

(a form of John)

> *Pronunciation Guide*
> Today: **jan´nah**

. . . which was the son of Janna . . . .
Luke 3:24

69

James

(a variation of Jacob)

> *Pronunciation Guide*
> Today: **jāmz**

And he taketh with him Peter and James and John, and began to be sore amazed, and to be very heavy; and saith unto them, . . . tarry ye here, and watch.

Mark 14:33-34

70

Jedidah

beloved, amiable

> *Pronunciation Guide*
> Today: **Je dī´dah**

And his [Josiah's] mother's name was
Jedidah . . . . *2 Kings 22:1*

71

Jamin*

right hand

Pronunciation Guide
Today: ja′min or ja mēēn′

. . . of Jamin, the family of the Jaminites . . . .
Numbers 26:12

72

Jemima

dove, handsome as the day

> *Pronunciation Guide*
> Bible: **yemīmāh**
> Today: **jə mī′mə**

And he [Job] called the name of the first,
Jemima . . . .   *Job 42:14*

73

Jason

healer

> *Pronunciation Guide*
> Bible: **Iāson**
> Today: **Jās´ən**

And when they found them not, they drew Jason . . . unto the rulers of the city, crying, These that have turned the world upside down are come hither also; whom Jason hath received. *Acts 17:6-7*

Joanna

the grace or mercy of God

And certain women, which had been
healed . . . Joanna the wife of Chuza
Herod's steward . . . .   *Luke 8:2-3*

75

Jered

descent

Pronunciation Guide
Today: **jair´ed**

Adam, Sheth, Enosh, Kenan, Mahalaleel,
Jered . . . . [Adam's line to Noah]
1 Chronicles 1:1-2

76

Joppa

beauty, comeliness

Pronunciation Guide
Today: **Jop´ah**

I was in the city of Joppa praying; and in a
trance I saw a vision . . . .   *Acts 11:5*

Jeremiah/Jeremy

whom Jehovah has appointed

Pronunciation Guide

Bible: **yirmeyāh**

Today: **jer´ə mī´ə; jər´ə mē**

. . . Before thou camest forth out of the womb I sanctified thee, and I ordained thee a prophet unto the nations.

Jeremiah 1:5

78

*Jordan**

flowing down

> *Pronunciation Guide*
> Today: **jor´d´n**

And it came to pass in those days, that
Jesus came from Nazareth of Galilee,
and was baptized of John in Jordan.

Mark 1:9

79

Jesse

to be, my present

> *Pronunciation Guide*
> Bible: **yīshaI**
> Today: **jes´ē**

. . . There is son born to Naomi; and they called his name Obed: he is the father of Jesse, the father of David.   *Ruth 4:17*

80

Judith

praised

> **Pronunciation Guide**
> Bible: **yehūdhīth**
> Today: **jōō′dith**

And Esau was forty years old when he took to wife Judith . . . . *Genesis 26:34*

81

Job

---

he that cries out of a hollow place

> *Pronunciation Guide*
> Bible: **Iyyōbh**
> Today: **jōb**

There was a man in the land of Uz, whose name was Job; and that man was perfect and upright, and one that feared God . . . .

Job 1:1

*J*ulia

downy

Salute Philologus, and Julia,... and all
the saints which are with them.

Romans 16:15

83

Joel

the Lord is God

> *Pronunciation Guide*
> Bible: yō' ēl
> Today: jō´əl

The word of the LORD . . . came to Joel the
son of Pethuel . . . .   *Joel 1:1*

84

*Kallai**

swift

Pronunciation Guide
Today: **kal´ai, kal ai´**

And in the days of Joiakim were priests,
the chief of the fathers: . . . of Sallai,
Kallai . . . .   *Nehemiah 12:12, 20*

85

Johanan

God is gracious

Then all the captains of the forces, and Johanan the son of Kareah . . . said unto Jeremiah . . . Pray for us unto the LORD thy God, even for all this remnant. . . .

Jeremiah 42:1-2

Kezia

---

cassia (laurel)

> *Pronunciation Guide*
>
> Bible: qesī 'āh
> Today: kēēs'ē a, ke zī'ah

And he [Job] called the name . . . of the
second, Kezia . . . .   *Job 42:14*

87

John

Yahweh is gracious

> *Pronunciation Guide*
> Bible: **yehōhānān**
> Today: **jän**

When Jesus therefore saw his mother, and the disciple [John] standing by, whom he loved, he saith unto his mother, Woman, behold thy son! *John 19:26*

*Lael**

devoted to God

Pronunciation Guide
Today: **lay´el**

And the chief of the house of the father
of the Gershonites shall be Eliasaph the
son of Lael.   *Numbers 3:24*

89

Jonah/Jonas

a dove

Pronunciation Guide
Bible: **yōnāh**
Today: **jōˊnə, jōˊnəs**

For as Jonas was three days and three nights in the whale's belly; so shall the Son of man be three days and three nights in the heart of the earth. *Matthew 12:40*

Lasha

to call, anoint

> *Pronunciation Guide*
> Today: **lay´shah**

And the border of the Canaanites was
from Sidon . . . even unto Lasha.

Genesis 10:19

Jonathan

Yahweh has given

Pronunciation Guide
Bible: **yehōnāthān**
Today: **jän´ ə thən**

And Jonathan Saul's son arose, and went to David into the wood, and strengthened his hand in God. *1 Samuel 23:16*

92

Leah

languid, gazelle

Pronunciation Guide
Today: lē′ə

. . . The LORD make the woman that is
come into thine house like Rachel and
like Leah, which two did build the house
of Israel . . . . *Ruth 4:11*

93

Joseph

may he add

And the patriarchs, moved with envy, sold
Joseph into Egypt: but God was with him,
and delivered him out of all his afflictions
. . . .   *Acts 7:9-10*

94

Lois

(Timothy's grandmother)

> *Pronunciation Guide*
> Today: lō′is

The unfeigned faith that is in thee, which dwelt first in thy grandmother Lois . . . . *2 Timothy 1:15*

95

Joshua

help of Jehovah

> *Pronunciation Guide*
> Bible: **yehōshū 'a**
> Today: **jăsh´oo wə**

And Joshua said unto the people, Ye are witnesses against yourselves that ye have chosen you the LORD, to serve him . . . .

Joshua 24:24

96

Lydia

(a seller of purple)

Pronunciation Guide
Today: **lid´ē ə**

And a certain woman named Lydia, a seller of purple, of the city of Thyatira ... heard us: whose heart the Lord opened ....
Acts 16:14

97

Judah

praised

> *Pronunciation Guide*
> Bible: **yehūdāh**
> Today: **joo′də**

Judah, thou art he whom thy brethren shall praise: . . . thy father's children shall bow down before thee.   *Genesis 49:8*

98

Mahlah

---

melodious song

And Zelophehad . . . had no sons, but
daughters: and the names of the
daughters . . . were Mahlah . . . .

Numbers 26:33

99

Levi

joining

Pronunciation Guide	
Bible:	lēwī
Today:	lēʹvī

And she [Leah] . . . bare a son; and said; . . . because I have born him three sons: there-fore was his name called Levi.

Genesis 29:34

100

Martha

lady

Then said Martha unto Jesus, . . . whatsoever thou wilt ask of God, God will give it thee. *John 11:21-22*

101

Linus

flax

Eubulus greeteth thee, and Pudens, and
Linus . . . .   *2 Timothy 4:21*

102

Mary

rebellion

And the angel said unto her, Fear not,
Mary: for thou hast found favour with
God. *Luke 1:30*

103

Lucas/Luke

of or belonging to Lucania

> *Pronunciation Guide*
> Today: lo͞ok /lo͞o′ kəs

Only Luke is with me.   *2 Timothy 4:11*

104

Merab

---

one who fights

> Pronunciation Guide
> Today: **mer´ab**

But it came to pass at the time when
Merab Saul's daughter should have been
given to David, that she was given to
Adriel.... *1 Samuel 18:19*

105

Malachi

the messenger of Jehovah

> *Pronunciation Guide*
> Today: **mal´ak ī**

The burden of the word of the LORD to Israel by Malachi. *Malachi 1:1*

106

*Mesha**

deliverance

And Mesha king of Moab was a sheep-
master . . . .   *2 Kings 3:4*

107

Mark/Marcus

polite, shining

> *Pronunciation Guide*
> Today: mark / mark´əs

108

The church that is at Babylon, elected together with you, saluteth you; and so doth
Marcus my son. *1 Peter 5:13*

Michal

brook

And David sent messengers to Ishbosheth
Saul's son, saying, Deliver me my wife
Michal . . . .   *2 Samuel 3:14*

Matthew

gift of God

> Pronunciation Guide
> Bible: **māttīthyāh**
> Today: **math´ yoo**

And as Jesus passed forth from thence, he saw a man, named Matthew, sitting at the receipt of custom: and he saith unto him, Follow me. *Matthew 9:9*

110

Miriam

---

rebellion

> *Pronunciation Guide*
> Today: **mir′ē am**

And Miriam the prophetess, the sister of
Aaron, took a timbrel in her hand; and
all the women went out after her with
timbrels and with dances.

Exodus 15:20

Micah/Michah

who is like God

> *Pronunciation Guide*
> Bible: **mīkhā(yah)**
> Today: **mī′kə**

Micah the Morasthite prophesied in the days of Hezekiah king of Judah, and spake to all the people of Judah . . . .

Jeremiah 26:18

Moriah

---

provided by Jehovah

> Pronunciation Guide
> Today: **mor ī´ah**

And he said, Take now thy son, thine
only son Isaac, whom thou lovest, and
get thee into the land of Moriah . . . .
Genesis 22:2

Michael

who is like God

> *Pronunciation Guide*
> Bible: **mīkhā' ēl**
> Today: **mī´k'l**

114

Yet Michael the archangel, when contend-
ing with the devil . . . said, The Lord rebuke
thee. *Jude 9*

Myra/Mirah

balsam

Pronunciation Guide
Today: mī′rə

And when we had sailed over the sea of Cilicia and Pamphylia, we came to Myra, a city of Lycia. *Acts 27:5*

115

Mishael

Who is what God is?

> Pronunciation Guide
> Today: **mish´ā el**

And the sons of Uzziel; Mishael . . . .
Exodus 6:22

116

Naomi

pleasant, my delight

> *Pronunciation Guide*
> Today: **na ō′mē**

And the women said unto Naomi,
Blessed be the LORD, which hath not
left thee this day without a kinsman,
that his name may be famous in Israel.
Ruth 4:14

117

Moses

___

saved from the water, child, son

Pronunciation Guide
Bible: **mōshēh**
Today: **mō´ziz**

And Moses stretched out his hand over the sea; and the LORD caused the sea to go back by a strong east wind all that night, and made the sea dry land, and the waters were divided. *Exodus 14:21*

Neah

(a city in the tribe of Zebulun)

> Pronunciation Guide
> Today: **nē´ah**

And their border . . . from thence
passeth on along to the east . . . and
goeth out to Remmon-methoar to
Neah.   *Joshua 19:11, 13*

119

Nathan/Nathanael

gift / gift of God

> *Pronunciation Guide*
> Today: **nā'thən, nə than'yəl**

120

Jesus saw Nathanael coming to him, and saith of him, Behold an Israelite indeed, in whom is no guile! *John 1:47*

Persis

the beloved

> *Pronunciation Guide*
> Today: **per´sis**

Salute the beloved Persis, which
laboured much in the Lord.

Romans 16:12

121

Nicolas/Nicholas

conqueror of the people

> *Pronunciation Guide*
> Bible: **Nikolaos**
> Today: **nik´ 'l əs**

122

. . . The whole multitude . . . chose . . .
Nicolas a proselyte of Antioch.   *Acts 6:5*

Phebe/Phoebe

---

the moon

Pronunciation Guide
Today: fē′ bē

I commend unto you Phebe our sister,
which is a servant of the church which
is at Cenchrea.   *Romans 16:1*

123

Noah

rest, comfort

> *Pronunciation Guide*
> Today: nō′ə

And God blessed Noah and his sons, and said unto them, Be fruitful and multiply, and replenish the earth.   *Genesis 9:1*

124

Prisca/Priscilla

ancient

Pronunciation Guide
Today: **pris´ca, pri sil´ə**

. . . Paul . . . came to Corinth and found
a certain Jew named Aquila, . . . and his
wife Priscilla . . . and . . . he abode with
them, . . . for . . . they were tentmakers.
Acts 18:1-3

125

Paul

little

Pronunciation Guide	
Bible:	**Paulus**
Today:	**pôl**

Then Paul answered, . . . I am ready not to be bound only, but also to die at Jerusalem for the name of the Lord Jesus.

Acts 21:13

Rachel

ewe

Pronunciation Guide
Bible: rāhēl
Today: rā´chəl

And Jacob served seven years for
Rachel; and they seemed unto him but
a few days, for the love he had to her.
Genesis 29:20

127

Peter

a rock

Pronunciation Guide
Bible: **Petra/Petros**
Today: **pēt′ər**

Then Peter said, Silver and gold have I none;
but such as I have give I thee.

Acts 3:6

128

Rebekah/Rebecca

quarrel appeased

> *Pronunciation Guide*
> Bible: **ribbqāh**
> Today: **ri bek´ə**

And Isaac loved Esau, because he did eat of his venison: but Rebekah loved Jacob. *Genesis 25:28*

129

Philip

lover of horses

> *Pronunciation Guide*
> Bible: **Philippos**
> Today: **fil´əp**

Have I been so long time with you, and yet hast thou not known me, Philip? he that hath seen me hath seen the Father.

John 14:9

Rhoda

a rose

> *Pronunciation Guide*
> Today: **rō´də**

And as Peter knocked at the door of the gate, a damsel came to hearken, named Rhoda. *Acts 12:13*

131

Reuben

behold, a son

Pronunciation Guide
Today: **roo′bin**

And Reuben answered them [his brothers], saying, Spake I not unto you, saying, Do not sin against the child; and ye would not hear?   *Genesis 42:22*

Ruth

companion

> Pronunciation Guide
> Bible: rē' uth
> Today: rōōth

And Ruth said, Intreat me not to leave
thee, or to return from following after
thee . . . . *Ruth 1:16*

Samson

---

like the sun

> *Pronunciation Guide*
> Bible: **shimshōn**
> Today: **sam´s'n**

And Samson said, Let me die with the Philis-
tines. And he bowed himself with all his might;
and the house fell upon . . .all the people that
were therein. *Judges 16:30*

Salome

---

perfect

Pronunciation Guide
Today: sə lō´mē

And when the sabbath was past, Mary Magdalene, and Mary the mother of James, and Salome, had bought sweet spices, that they might come and anoint him.   *Mark 16:1*

135

Samuel

---

name of God

Pronunciation Guide
Bible: shĕmū'ēl
Today: sam'yoo wəl

And Samuel grew, and the LORD was with him, and did let none of his words fall to the ground. *1 Samuel 3:19*

136

Sarah/Sara

---

princess

> *Pronunciation Guide*
> Today: **ser´ə**

. . .Sarah shall her name be. And I will bless her . . . and she shall be a mother of nations; kings of people shall be of her. *Genesis 17:15-16*

137

Saul

asked for

Pronunciation Guide
Bible: **shā' ūl**
Today: **sôl**

And when Samuel saw Saul, the LORD said unto him, Behold the man whom I spake to thee of! this same shall reign over my people. *1 Samuel 9:17*

138

Sharon

a field, a song

I am the rose of Sharon, and the lily of the valleys.   *Song of Solomon 2:1*

139

Seth

appointed

> *Pronunciation Guide*
> Today: **seth**

. . . And she [Eve] bare a son, and called his name Seth: For God, said she, hath appointed me another seed instead of Abel . . . .

Genesis 4:25

Sherah

affinity

Pronunciation Guide
Today: **sher´ah**

And his [Beriah's] daughter was Sherah,
who built Beth-horon the nether . . . .
1 Chronicles 7:24

141

Silas

asked for

Pronunciation Guide	
Bible:	sh' îlà
Today:	sī las

And at midnight Paul and Silas prayed, and sang praises unto God: and the prisoners heard them. *Acts 16:25*

142

Shiloh *

peace, abundance

Pronunciation Guide
Today: shi´lō

And the whole congregation of the children of Israel assembled together at Shiloh, . . . and the land was subdued before them. *Joshua 18:1*

143

Simon

---

heard, a hearkening

> *Pronunciation Guide*
> Bible: **shim ʻōn**
> Today: **sī´mən**

Is not this the carpenter, the son of Mary,
the brother of James, . . . and Simon?

Mark 6:3

144

Shiphrah

beauty

Pronunciation Guide
Today: **shif´rah**

And the king of Egypt spake to the Hebrew midwives, of which the name of the one was Shiphrah . . . .

Exodus 1:15

145

Solomon

peaceable

Pronunciation Guide

Bible: **shĕlōmōh**
Today: **säl´ə mən**

And God gave Solomon wisdom and understanding exceeding much, and largeness of heart, even as the sand that is on the sea shore. *1 Kings 4:29*

146

Susanna

lily

Pronunciation Guide	
Bible:	**shōshannāh**
Today:	**sōo zan′ə**

. . . And Susanna, and many others . . . ministered unto him [Jesus] of their substance. *Luke 8:3*

147

Stephen/Stephanas

crowned

Pronunciation Guide
Today: stē´vən, ste fan´əs

And Stephen, full of faith and power, did great wonders and miracles among the people. *Acts 6:8*

148

Tabitha

gazelle

Pronunciation Guide
Today: **tab´ith ah**

Now there was at Joppa a certain disciple named Tabitha. . .this woman was full of good works and almsdeeds which she did. *Acts 9:36*

149

Thomas

a twin

Then saith he [Jesus] to Thomas, Reach
hither thy finger, and behold my hands;
and reach hither thy hand, and thrust it
into my side: and be not faithless, but
believing. *John 20:27*

150

*T*amar

a palm tree

Pronunciation Guide
Today: **ta′mar or ta mar′**

And unto Absalom there were born three sons, and one daughter, whose name was Tamar: she was a woman of a fair countenance.   *2 Samuel 14:27*

151

Timothy

honoring God

Now if Timotheus come, see that he may
be with you without fear: for he worketh
the work of the Lord . . . .

1 Corinthians 16:10

152

*T*arah

(an Israelite encampment in the wilderness)

Pronunciation Guide
Today: **tare′ah**

And they departed from Tahath, and
pitched at Tarah. *Numbers 33:27*

153

Tobiah

Jehovah is good

The children of Delaiah, the children of Tobiah, the children of Nekoda, six hundred fifty and two.   *Ezra 2:60*

154

Vashti

---

beautiful

> *Pronunciation Guide*
> Today: **vash´tē**

. . . The king . . . commanded . . . to bring Vashti the queen before the king with the crown royal . . . for she was fair to look on. *Esther 1:10-11*

155

Zachariah/Zachary

whom Jehovah remembers

> *Pronunciation Guide*
>
> Bible: **zeharyah**
> Today: **zak′ə rī′ə / zak′ər ē**

And Jeroboam slept with his fathers, even with the kings of Israel; and Zachariah his son reigned in his stead.   *2 Kings 14:29*